The Little Book of
HEALTHY HABITS

By Zack Bush and Laurie Friedman
Illustrated by Sarah Van Evera

THIS BOOK BELONGS TO:

_____

Copyright © 2023 Publishing Power, LLC
All Rights Reserved
All inquiries about this book can be sent
to the author at info@thelittlebookof.com
Published in the United States by Publishing Power, LLC
ISBN: 978-1-959141-18-1
For more information, visit our website:
www.BooksByZackAndLaurie.com
Paperback

HEALTHY HABITS.
What are they and why are they important?

There's so much to know about **HEALTHY HABITS** and how to make them part of your everyday routine.

Ready to learn more? Just turn the page.

HABITS are things that you do on a regular basis.

HEALTHY HABITS are things you do—day after day—that are good for your body, your mind, and your soul.

HEALTHY HABITS are important because they help you grow up strong, healthy, and happy.

You weren't born with **HEALTHY HABITS.**
Babies have to be taught to do things as they grow.

But now that you're big, there are so many **HEALTHY HABITS** you can learn and make a part of your daily life. Let's talk about some of them!

Eating foods that are good for your body is one of the most important **HEALTHY HABITS.**

That means choosing fresh foods like fruits and vegetables, whole grain products like wheat bread, and healthy proteins like fish or chicken.

These foods are much healthier for you than junk food such as candy and chips.

Ready for a fun quiz to see how much you know about making healthy food choices?

WHICH ONE IS HEALTHIER?

FRUIT vs. CANDY

PIE vs. VEGETABLES

HOT DOG vs. FISH

SALAD vs. BURGER

What you eat matters, but so does when you eat.

Eating a good breakfast is a **HEALTHY HABIT** that will give you energy for the day ahead and help you stay more focused in school.

What you drink is important too. Water is much healthier for you than sodas and juices, which are full of sugar.

Drinking plenty of water is a **HEALTHY HABIT** that will keep you hydrated, feeling good, and having fun.

Another **HEALTHY HABIT** that you can incorporate into your life is exercise.

Moving your body is fun and feels good, but it also has many health benefits.

When you exercise you will feel calmer, happier, and more productive. You will even sleep better at night!

When it comes to exercise, there are so many fun ways to move. What do you like to do?

SWIM  RUN

BIKE HIKE

SKATE

THROW

DANCE
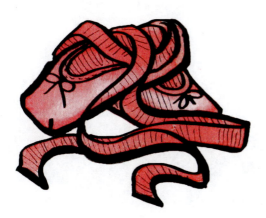

CLIMB

Keeping your body clean is another very important **HEALTHY HABIT.**

So is . . .

Brushing your teeth.

Washing your hands.

Going to the doctor.

And the dentist too.

When you take care of your body, you will stay healthier and be able to do the things that you enjoy, like playing outside and having fun with your friends.

Another **HEALTHY HABIT** that is really good for you is going to bed on time. Getting enough sleep will help you wake up feeling refreshed and ready for the day ahead!

Making **HEALTHY HABITS** part of your life might feel weird or unfamiliar at first. But the more you do something, the more it will feel like a regular part of your routine.

Ready to learn about a few more healthy habits? Keeping your room clean is a great **HEALTHY HABIT.** When your personal space is neat and organized, you will feel better and more productive.

You will feel good and have fun when you are with people you care about and who care about you.

Spending time in nature is another **HEALTHY HABIT** that will make you feel good.

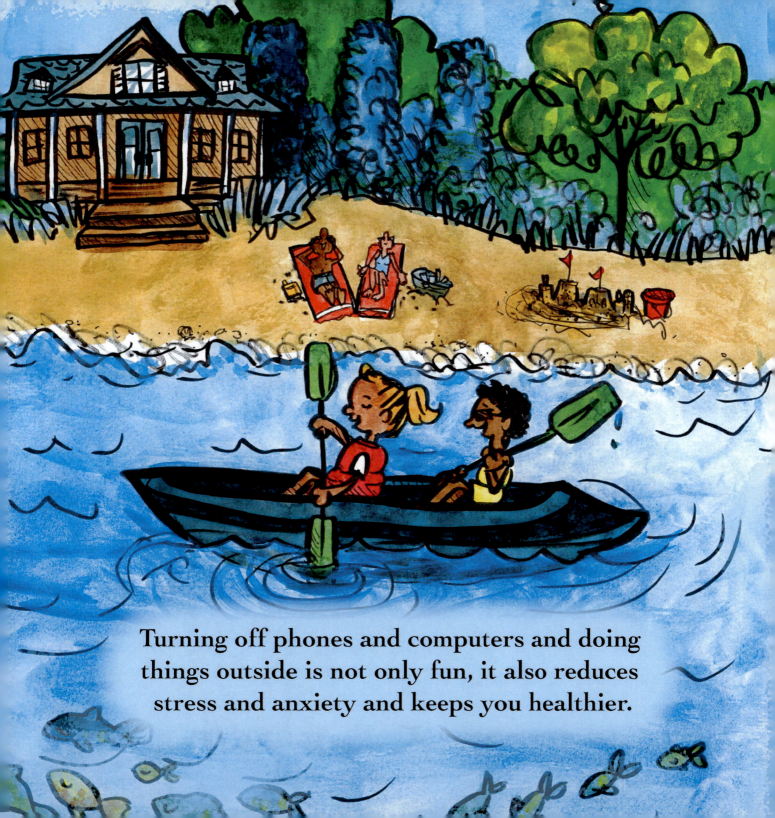

Turning off phones and computers and doing things outside is not only fun, it also reduces stress and anxiety and keeps you healthier.

Smiling more and giving hugs are two small but powerful **HEALTHY HABITS** that not only help reduce stress but also make you less likely to get sick.

So go ahead . . .
start smiling and hugging today!

One of the single most important **HEALTHY HABITS** that you can have is to try and keep a positive attitude.

It's easy to get discouraged when things don't go your way.

But try to stay positive and remind yourself that you are strong and smart and can get through challenges.

And remember . . .
no one is perfect. If you have
a day when your **HABITS**
aren't so healthy, don't worry.
Just wake up tomorrow and
begin again!

And when you do something good and healthy, be sure to take a moment and celebrate yourself.

You can even keep a list of **HEALTHY HABITS** you would like to incorporate into your life.

Which HEALTHY HABITS will you start practicing?

CONGRATULATIONS!

Now you know so much about
HEALTHY HABITS.

Go to the website www.BooksByZackAndLaurie.com
and print out your badges from the
Printables & Activities page.
And if you like this book,
please go to Amazon and leave a kind review.

Other books in the series include:

SOCIAL/EMOTIONAL/VALUES
The Little Book of Kindness
The Little Book of Patience
The Little Book of Confidence
The Little Book of Positivity
The Little Book of Love
The Little Book of Responsibility
The Little Book of Curiosity
The Little Book of Gratitude
The Little Book of Friendship
The Little Book of Laughter
The Little Book of Creativity
The Little Book of Honesty
The Little Book of Imagination
The Little Book of Happiness

ACTIVITIES/IDEAS
The Little Book of Camping
The Little Book of Sports
The Little Book of Music
The Little Book of Transportation
The Little Book of Government

The Little Book of the Supreme Court
The Little Book of Presidential Elections
The Little Book of Grandparents
The Little Book of Bedtime
The Little Book of Good Manners
The Little Book of Good Deeds
The Little Book of Yoga

SCIENCE/NATURAL WORLD
The Little Book of Nature
The Little Book of Outer Space
The Little Book of Going Green
The Little Book of Pets
The Little Book of Dinosaurs
The Little Book of Weather

MILESTONES/HOLIDAYS
The Little Book of Kindergarten
The Little Book of First Grade
The Little Book of Valentine's Day
The Little Book of Father's Day
The Little Book of Halloween
The Little Book of Giving (Holiday Edition)
The Little Book of Santa Claus

Made in United States
North Haven, CT
09 October 2024